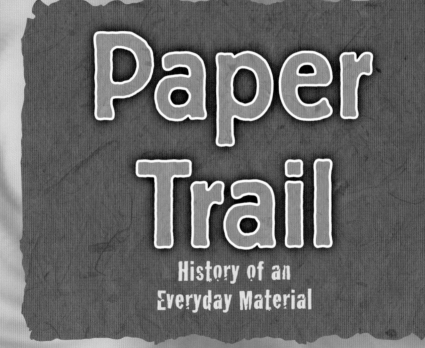

Paper Trail

History of an Everyday Material

Library of Congress Cataloging-in-Publication Data

Brocker, Susan.
   Paper trail : history of an everyday material / by Susan Brocker.
       p. cm. -- (Shockwave)
   Includes and index.
   ISBN-10: 0-531-17589-8 (lib. bdg.)
   ISBN-13: 978-0-531-17589-7 (lib. bdg.)
   ISBN-10: 0-531-18817-5 (pbk.)
   ISBN-13: 978-0-531-18817-0 (pbk.)
1. Papermaking--Juvenile literature. I. Title. II. Series.

  TS1105.5.B73 2008
  676--dc22

  2007014446

Published in 2008 by Children's Press, an imprint of Scholastic Inc.,
557 Broadway, New York, New York 10012
www.scholastic.com

08 09 10 11 12 13 14 15 16 17
10 9 8 7 6 5 4 3 2 1

Printed in China through Colorcraft Ltd., Hong Kong

Author: Susan Brocker
Educational Consultant: Ian Morrison
Editor: Nerida Frost
Design and Diagrams: Miguel Carvajal
Photo Researcher: Jamshed Mistry

Photographs by: AKG Images (p. 15); **Big Stock Photo** (p. 11); **Courtesy of eREAD** (electronic
book device, p. 30); **Courtesy of Plastic Logic** (flexible electronic display, p. 31); **DIGITAL IMAGE
© 2007, The Museum of Modern Art/Scala, Florence** (Bubbles Chaise Longue by Frank O. Gehry,
1987, p. 21); **Ingram Image Library** (p. 3; p. 5; harvesting, p. 29; logging truck, pp. 32–33);
Jennifer and Brian Lupton (teenagers, pp. 32–33); **Photolibrary** (pp. 8–9; clay tablets, papyrus
strips, p. 11; pp. 12–14; wasp nest; de Réaumur observing insects, pp. 16–17; p. 19; papier-mâché
dogs, pp. 22–23; p. 24; untreated waste water, p. 25; stacks of paper, p. 26; p. 28; burn-off, p. 29);
Robert J. Lang (origami beetle, p. 23); **Tom Curry** (papercrete house, p. 20); **Tranz/Corbis** (cover;
man with papyrus, pp. 10–11; papermaking machines, p. 17; girl with origami, p. 23; paper mill,
p. 25; tying up papers, p. 27; girl with laptop, pp. 30–31)

All illustrations and other photographs © Weldon Owen Education Inc.

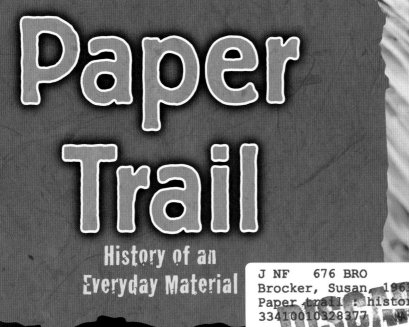

Paper Trail

History of an Everyday Material

Susan Brocker

children's press®

An imprint of Scholastic Inc.

NEW YORK • TORONTO • LONDON • AUCKLAND • SYDNEY
MEXICO CITY • NEW DELHI • HONG KONG
DANBURY, CONNECTICUT

CHECK THESE OUT!

SHOCKER
Stuff to Shock, Surprise, and Amaze You

Quick Recaps and Notable Notes

Word Stunners and Other Oddities

The Heads-Up on Expert Reading

Links to More Information

CONTENTS

absorbent (*ab ZOR buhnt*) having the ability to soak up liquids

digester a large vat filled with water and chemicals for making pulp in a paper mill

durable (*DUR uh buhl*) tough and long-lasting

kenaf (*kuh NAF*) a native plant of Africa that is grown for its fiber

papyrus (*puh PYE ruhss*) a reed-like water plant, or the paper-like writing material made from it

plantation a farm where usually one particular crop is being grown

pulp (*PUHLP*) a soft, mushy mixture that has most of the liquid squeezed out of it

renewable from a source that can never be used up, or that can be replaced

For additional vocabulary, see Glossary on page 34.

Digester is an interesting word. Wood chips are broken down into pulp in the digester just as food is broken down, or *digested*, in our stomachs!

Modern Egyptian painting on a sheet of papyrus

7

We use paper every day. We write on it, read from it, and wrap our food in it. We even blow our noses on it! What is paper? You may know that paper is made from wood. Did you know that paper can also be made out of old rags and fishing nets?

Paper comes from the long, stringy threads, called fibers, found in plants and trees. The fibers are beaten and mixed with water to make a mushy **pulp**. The pulp is then flattened and dried to form sheets of paper.

There are many different types of paper and many different uses for it. Paper can be smooth and glossy for making posters, cards, and magazines. It can be soft and **absorbent** for making tissues, towels, and diapers. It can be strong and hard for making boxes, packaging, and even furniture. The properties of paper depend on the fibers and processes used to make it.

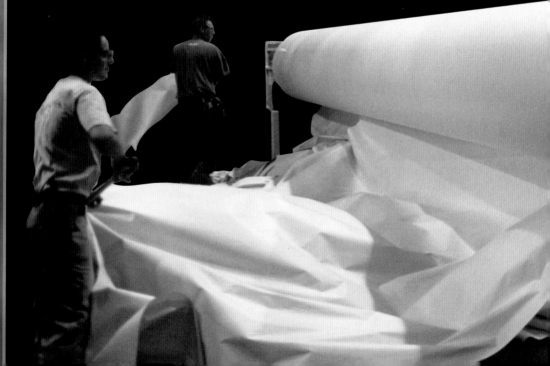

World Use of Printed Paper

Books
2.3%

Periodicals
3.7%

Newspapers
8.5%

Office documents
85.5%

Before Paper

Imagine reading books made from leaves, or using heavy clay tablets for writing. Before paper was invented, people wrote on just about anything. They wrote on cave walls, pieces of pottery, bone, silk, wood, and wax.

The ancient Egyptians wrote on a material they made from a reed-like plant called **papyrus**. They crisscrossed thin strips of the reeds. Then they pounded them together into flat sheets. They glued the sheets together and rolled them into scrolls. Paper gets its name from papyrus.

The heading and first sentence clearly indicate what these pages are about. This sure makes reading easier.

Beginning in about 200 B.C., the people of ancient Greece and western Asia used parchment for writing. It was made of animal skins that were cleaned, soaked, and stretched. Then they were rubbed with chalk and **pumice** to make them smooth. Parchment was popular in Europe in the **Middle Ages**, until the invention of printing in 1440 A.D.

Papyrus grows along the Nile River. People in Egypt today still use it to make writing material.

Five thousand years ago, in **Mesopotamia**, people wrote on clay tablets. Symbols were written in wet clay, which hardened when dried.

In Mexico, the Otomi (*Oh TOE mee*) people have been making a paper-like material out of bark, probably since the 1500s.

Up until about 600 A.D., Japanese people wrote on silk. However, it was too expensive for widespread use.

Beginning in about 500 B.C., people in southeast Asia used palm leaves for writing. They cut the leaves into long strips and **etched** writing into them. They strung the leaves together to make books.

Papyrus strips

11

Secret Art

America
1690 A.D.

To make paper out of papyrus, people had to stick or weave the reeds together. In about 100 A.D., Ts'ai Lun (*TZEYE Lun*) of China discovered a way to make plant fibers "weave themselves." Ts'ai Lun soaked tree bark, old rags, and **hemp** fishing nets in water. He mashed the mixture into a pulp. Then he pressed out the liquid. He left a layer of pulp to dry in the sun. When it had dried, the plant fibers had matted together. Paper as we know it was born!

The Chinese kept the art of papermaking a secret for about 500 years. From China, papermaking spread to Korea and Japan. Then it followed the **Silk Road** to Central Asia and the Middle East. From there, it went to Spain with the **Moors**. Soon papermaking spread throughout Europe. The first paper mill was set up in England in about 1488. About 200 years later, the first paper mill in America opened in Philadelphia.

As I was reading this page, I found myself looking over at the map. It really helped me to see how the use of paper spread from east to west.

Ts'ai Lun was an official at the Imperial Chinese Court. Here he is shown **supervising** workers making paper.

1. Bark, hemp, and rags were boiled into a pulp.
2. A frame of reeds was dipped into the pulp. The pulp on the frame was dried in the sun. Then the sheet of paper was lifted off the frame.

England
1488 A.D.

Germany
1400 A.D.

Italy
1200 A.D.

Spain
1150 A.D.

Baghdad
795 A.D.

China
100 A.D.

Korea
600 A.D.

Morocco
1100 A.D.

Damascus
900 A.D.

Samarqand
751 A.D.

Japan
610 A.D.

1.

How Pulp Becomes Paper

To make paper, fibers are mashed into a pulp. This flattens the fibers, increasing the area of contact between them when they dry. The pulp is spread in a thin layer to dry and the fibers bond together in a tight weave. This creates a solid sheet of paper.

Magnified bathroom-tissue fibers

Magnified magazine-paper fibers

Before Pulping

Small contact area

After Pulping

Larger contact area

13

Rags to Riches

In the beginning, Europeans made paper out of rags, as the Chinese had done. A huge rag trade developed. Rag pickers sorted the clothes by color and condition. They removed buttons and hooks. Then they cut the rags into strips. They wet the strips and rolled them into balls. The rags were left to soak for a few weeks before being made into paper.

Papermaking was a slow and messy process. Papermakers spent 12 hours a day in dark, damp rooms. They worked with their arms deep in pulpy, smelly water. The demand for paper grew, as more and more people learned to read and write. It became harder to find enough rags. There was a constant shortage of them in the 1800s. People began to search for new, easier methods of making paper.

SHOCKER

In the 1800s, some American papermakers imported Egyptian **mummies** into the United States. They used the linen wrappings from the mummies to make pulp!

Making Paper

- rag pickers bought old clothes
- clothes were then sorted
- hooks and buttons were removed
- clothes were cut into strips
- rags were soaked for a few weeks
- paper was produced

Rag pickers traveled from door to door buying old clothes.

Spreading the Word

In 1798, a Frenchman named Nicholas Louis Robert invented the first papermaking machine. It produced paper in long, unbroken strips wound onto rollers. Machine-made paper soon replaced single sheets of paper made by hand.

The next breakthrough in papermaking came in the mid-1800s. A French **naturalist** named René de Réaumur was observing wasps making their nests. He saw that they chewed up tiny bits of wood into a mushy pulp. The wasps molded the pulp into paper nests. This gave de Réaumur the idea to use wood fibers to make paper.

There was no shortage of wood at the time. At last, there was a ready supply of fibers for making paper quickly and cheaply. The printing press had been invented in 1440. These two inventions enabled many more people to get books and newspapers than in the past. Information became available to a larger part of society. As more people learned to read and write, they used their increased knowledge to bring about social change.

De Réaumur observing insects

16

Early Paper Machine

The Fourdrinier (*Foor druh NEER*) brothers of England improved on Nicholas Robert's invention. Their papermaking machine went into operation in England in 1803. Modern papermaking machines still work on the same principles as their machine. To this day, they are known as Fourdrinier machines.

Early papermaking machine

Modern papermaking machine

The pronunciation guide for words such as *Fourdrinier* is really useful. It shows how many syllables there are, how each is pronounced, and which syllable is stressed.

Paper Mills

Today, we make most of our paper from wood pulp. Trees are cut down. Logs are taken to the mill. Here they are chipped into tiny pieces. The chips are "cooked" in water and chemicals to make a gooey pulp. Additives, such as starch and clay, are mixed into the pulp. These improve the strength and quality of the paper. Next the pulp is bleached or dyed. Then it is pressed and dried to form paper.

The quality and type of the paper produced depend on the fibers and processes used to make it. Glossy paper is coated with starch and clay, and polished with rollers. Waterproof paper has a thin coating of wax. Newsprint is made from wood pulp that is not given any special treatment. It is cheap and easy to make, but yellows with age.

Turning Trees Into Paper

1. The trees are cut down. The logs are transported to a paper mill.

2. A spinning drum, called the debarker, strips the bark off the logs.

3. A chipper cuts the logs into small pieces.

4. In the **digester**, the wood chips are mixed with water and chemicals. They are cooked into a pulp.

Mountain of wood chips at a mill

SHOCKER

In one week, a modern papermaking machine can make a sheet of paper long enough to stretch across the Atlantic Ocean!

A technician tests a sample of bleached pulp from a pulp-drying roller.

5. In the washers, the pulp is cleaned and blended with additives.

6. The headbox regulates the flow of pulp onto a moving metal screen, called the wire.

9. Heated cylinders finish drying the pulp. As it dries, the fibers bond, forming paper.

8. The rollers squeeze more water out of the mat.

10. The paper is pressed flat by metal rollers and wound onto large reels.

7. On the wire, the water drains out of the pulp. It leaves behind a mat of fibers.

Paper All Around

Look around you – our world is full of things made of paper. At school, there are books, magazines, newspapers, printer paper, and posters. At home, we may have cereal boxes, juice cartons, and grocery bags. We even use paper money!

Many goods we buy, such as shoes, are packed in cardboard boxes. Cardboard is made from sheets of paper pressed together. Big items, such as computers, are packed in **corrugated** cardboard. It is extra strong and protects the things inside from getting damaged.

Did you know that there are also clothes, furniture, and even houses made out of paper? Papercrete is a new building material. It is made up of water, cement, sand, and shredded newspapers. The mixture is poured into blocks and dried in the sun. When papercrete dries, it is as strong as wood or concrete. However, it will not burn or crack.

magazines

newspapers

printer paper

Paper

juice cartons

money

cereal boxes

Papercrete house in Texas

Money is printed on high-quality paper. Scraps of cloth are mixed into the wood pulp to make it **durable**.

Corrugated cardboard is made up of three layers of paper: a corrugated layer between two sheets of paper. The board is very strong because the inner layer is like a series of arches. Just like the arches in buildings, these arches can support a lot of weight.

Frank Gehry is an American **architect** who makes unusual furniture out of corrugated cardboard. This chair is in the design collection of the Museum of Modern Art in New York City.

21

Paper Art

As the invention of paper spread, people discovered different and fun ways of using it. Shortly after the invention of paper, people in China started folding paper into shapes. This hobby developed into an art form in Japan around 700 A.D. Origami means "folded paper" in Japanese. In those days, the Japanese created **traditional** figures, such as birds, flowers, and fish. Today, origami is popular all over the world. People now make origami bugs, dinosaurs, and even space rockets!

In about 1600, people started using papier mâché. This name means "chewed paper" in French. People mixed pieces of paper and glue together and molded it into any shape. When the finished product was painted and varnished, it became almost as hard as wood.

Origami animals

Papier-mâché dogs were popular in Japan in the 1600s.

SHOCKER

An early manufacturer of papier mâché in Europe employed two French women. He had them chew the paper for the papier mâché! This is how it got its French name.

Origami Artist and Scientist

**Origami beetle
by Robert J. Lang**

Robert J. Lang grew up in Atlanta, Georgia. Since he was small, he has folded pieces of paper into fantastic creatures and figures. His interest in origami made him want to understand the mathematics behind his art. As an adult, he became an engineer and a **laser physicist**.

Now Robert is a full-time origami artist. He also uses origami to solve practical problems. He has helped design space telescopes and air bags. But he still makes origami creatures, especially bugs, just for fun!

23

Paper Pollution

Unfortunately, the papermaking process is often very dirty. Paper mills can pollute the air, water, and land around them. They may use harmful chemicals, such as chlorine, to bleach wood pulp. Acids are often used to break down wood fibers. These chemicals get into the waste water from the mills. They can end up in our lakes and rivers.

Papermaking also uses huge numbers of trees. Fortunately, trees are a **renewable** resource. This means that once a tree is cut down another one can be planted in its place. Most of the wood used to make paper comes from special **plantations.** On plantations, trees are planted, harvested, and replanted. Plantations can yield three to four times as much wood as natural forests.

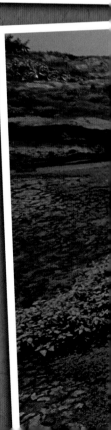

Some people are concerned about the lack of diversity of plant and animal life on plantations, compared with natural forests.

Paper mill in Virginia

The author has used the words *fortunately* and *unfortunately* in this text. These words help me to predict that some good and bad points are going to be made.

Untreated waste water from a paper mill

Precious Paper

People waste huge amounts of paper every day. We can reduce the amount of paper we use by cutting down on packaging. We can reuse many paper products, such as old envelopes, boxes, and bags. We can also recycle old paper instead of throwing it away. It can be turned into new paper.

Paper to be recycled is collected and sorted according to color and quality. The paper is shredded and pulped. The pulp is cleaned, removing ink or glue. Recycling paper uses less wood, water, and energy than making paper from pulp. Fewer chemicals are used, so it causes less pollution.

Make Your Own Recycled Paper

You will need: old paper, blotting paper, warm water, a piece of wire gauze about 6 inches by 6 inches, a bowl, an egg beater, a rolling pin

1. Rip the old paper into tiny pieces. Soak them in a bowl of warm water for at least 15 minutes.

2. Beat the paper into a pulp with the egg beater.

3. Dip the gauze into the pulp. Lift it up flat to drain off the water.

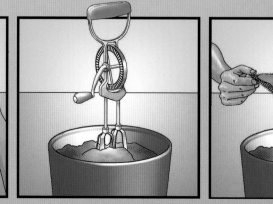

Stacks of old paper for recycling

The Three R's

- Reduce – the use of paper packaging
- Reuse – envelopes, boxes, and paper
- Recycle – old paper to make new paper

Did You Know?

Using one ton of recycled paper saves:

- 17 trees
- 300 gallons of oil
- 7,000 gallons of water
- 3 cubic yards of **landfill** space
- enough energy to heat a home for six months

4. Gently turn the gauze upside down over a sheet of blotting paper.

5. Remove the gauze. Put another piece of blotting paper on top.

6. Use the rolling pin to roll the sheets. When dry, take off the top sheet. Peel off your new recycled paper.

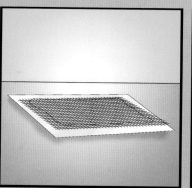

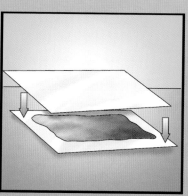

Planet-Friendly Paper

Today, paper manufacturers are trying to find ways to make paper without harming the environment. To reduce the number of trees cut down, many now reuse paper. They are also starting to use fibers other than wood to make pulp. Plants such as hemp, **kenaf**, bamboo, banana, and seaweed can all be used to make paper. Farm waste is also a good source of fiber for papermaking. Agri-pulp, as it is called, is made from the stalks of food crops, such as wheat, oats, barley, or sugar cane.

Many places now have strict laws regarding waste water and gases from paper mills. The mills must collect waste water in big tanks and clean it before returning it to rivers. They must fit their chimney stacks with filters to keep harmful gases from escaping into the air. Scientists are also developing ways to make paper without using so many harmful chemicals.

Kenaf provides three to five times more fiber per harvest than pine trees. Kenaf fiber is naturally whiter than wood, so it doesn't need to be bleached.

Every day, about sixty-two million newspapers are printed in the United States. Forty-four million are thrown away as soon as they are read. That's the **equivalent** of 500,000 trees being dumped into landfills each week!

In the past, stalks left in the fields after harvesting were burned off (left), causing pollution. Today, the stalks from food crops can be used to make agri-pulp.

A Paperless Society?

Can you imagine a world without paper? Some people believe that, one day, we may have a paperless society. Many people thought that computers would put an end to paper, but that hasn't happened. Instead, people use even more paper. Huge amounts of paper are used for printing and storing information from computers.

Today, many people have laptop computers. Yet many of us still write and draw with a pen and paper. Most of us also prefer to lie in bed or in a park with a book, instead of a laptop! However, what if computer screens felt and looked like paper and were just as light?

Some scientists believe that the days of paper books and newspapers are nearly over. Researchers are working to replace them with electronic paper. E-paper is a computer screen that is so thin and **flexible** that you can roll it up and put it in your pocket!

Electronic book device

Paperless Paper

Scientists are working to create an electronic display on a material that has the look and feel of paper. It can be erased, updated, and used over and over again. The battery-powered paper would be easy to read in bright sunlight or dark rooms.

One page could hold and display the contents of many books. People could download the daily newspaper or latest book onto a single sheet of e-paper. Scientists think we will be able to do this by 2015!

Flexible electronic display

31

...one of the world's most amazing and useful materials. It can be smooth, soft, strong, or hard. We can fold it and mold it into different shapes. We can use it to make all sorts of things.

But papermaking uses up trees and causes pollution. Many people are working hard to find ways to make and use paper that do not harm our environment.

WHAT DO YOU THINK?

Do you think people should be trying to create a paperless society?

PRO

I think we use too many trees and too much energy to make paper. Even if we use recycled paper and fewer chemicals, we still end up with huge amounts of paper in the garbage. In the long run, e-paper is a better solution.

At the same time, much time and money are being invested in developing the technology for a paperless society. Many scientists believe that this is the better solution for the world. It would be good for the environment. It could also give us amazing new possibilities for distributing and sharing information.

CON

Paper is made from a renewable resource. It is recyclable. Unlike materials such as plastic, it rots when we throw it away. We should keep trying to reduce the use of wood. If we clean up the process of papermaking as well, we can use paper for years to come.

GLOSSARY

architect (*AR kuh tekt*) a person who designs buildings

corrugated (*KOR oh gay tid*) shaped into ridges or ripples

equivalent (*ih KWIV uh lunt*) the same in shape, value, or importance

etch to engrave or draw on a surface, using a sharp object to cut into it

flexible able to bend without breaking

hemp a plant whose fibers are often used to make ropes and sacks

landfill an area where garbage is buried

laser a machine that produces a narrow, powerful beam of light of a particular wavelength

Mesopotamia (*Mehs uh puh TAY mee uh*) an ancient civilization in the Middle East

Middle Ages the period in European history from about 500 A.D. to about 1500 A.D.

Moors the people from northern Africa who invaded Spain in 711 A.D.

mummy a dead body that has been preserved

naturalist a person who studies nature

periodical a journal or magazine that is published at regular intervals

physicist (*FIZ i sist*) a scientist who studies the science of matter and energy (physics)

pumice (*PUHM iss*) a light volcanic rock that is used for smoothing and polishing

Samarqand (*SAHM uhr kahnd*) a city in what is now Uzbekistan

Silk Road the ancient overland trade route that connected Europe and Asia

supervise to watch over or direct a person or group of people

traditional done in an established and special way

Mummy

FIND OUT MORE

BOOKS

Atkinson, Mary. *What Do You Mean?: Communication Isn't Easy.*
  Scholastic Inc., 2008.

Barnett, Paul; Diefendorf, David; Greenstein, Ruth; Ng, Uechi; Ranieri,
  Tom; Prokos, Anna. *Conservation and Natural Resources.* Gareth Stevens
  Publishing, 2004.

Brookfield, Karen and Pordes, Laurence. *Book.* DK Eyewitness Books, 2000.

Harlow, Rosie and Morgan, Sally. *Garbage and Recycling.* Kingfisher, 2002.

Heinrichs, Ann. *The Printing Press.* Franklin Watts, 2005.

WEB SITES

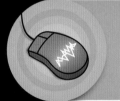

Go to the Web sites below
to learn more about the
history of paper.

www.historyforkids.org/learn/literature/paper.htm

www.paperonline.org

www.papiermache.co.uk

INDEX

ABOUT THE AUTHOR

Susan Brocker loves writing books for children of all ages, both fiction and nonfiction. She especially enjoys researching and discovering weird and wonderful facts from our past. For instance, she would never have believed that people once made paper out of the linen wrapped around Egyptian mummies! Susan is also a nature lover and was pleased to learn of the advances being made in papermaking to help protect our fragile planet.